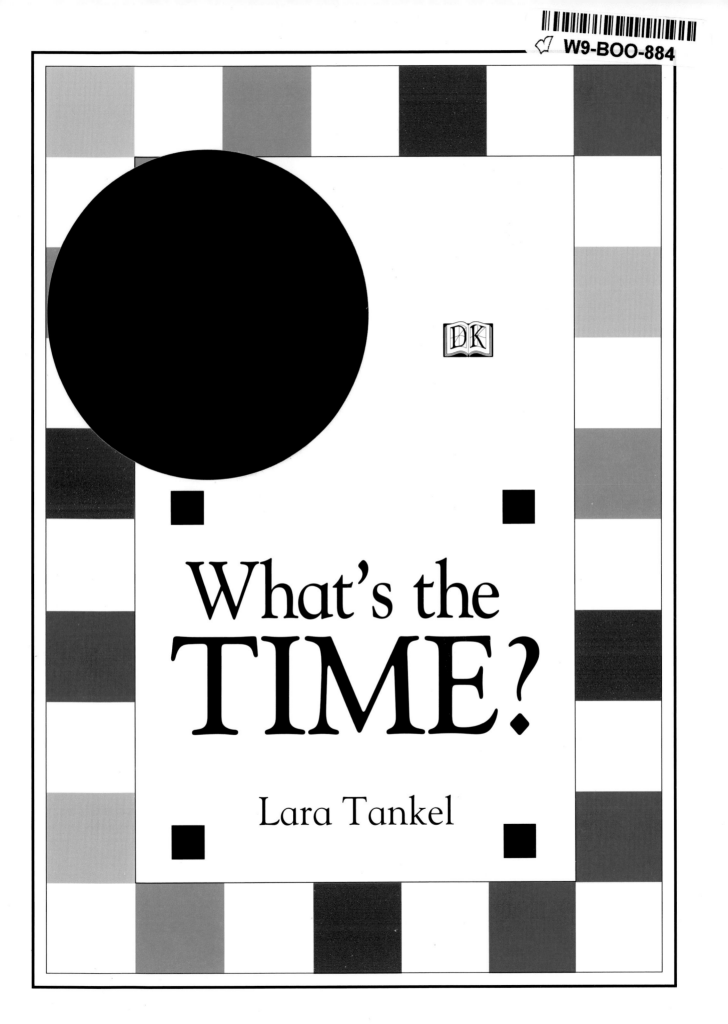

DK

What's the TIME?

Lara Tankel

A DK PUBLISHING BOOK

Managing Editor Sheila Hanly
Designer Mary Sandberg
Production Marguerite Fenn
U.S. Assistant Editor Camela Decaire

Photography Steve Shott,
Paul Bricknell, Dave King

First American Edition, 1995
2 4 6 8 10 9 7 5 3

Published in the United States by
DK Publishing Inc., 95 Madison Avenue
New York, New York 10016

Copyright © 1995 Dorling Kindersley Limited, London

Library of Congress Cataloging-in-Publication Data
Tankel, Lara. 1967–
What's the time? / written by Lara Tankel.
p. cm.
ISBN 1-56458-726-6
1. Time measurements – Juvenile literature. (1. Time. 2. Time
measurements.) I. Title.
QB213.T36 1994
529–dc20 –dc20
(529)   94-28972
                         CIP
                         AC
Color reproduction by Colourscan
Printed in Singapore by Tien Wah Press Ltd

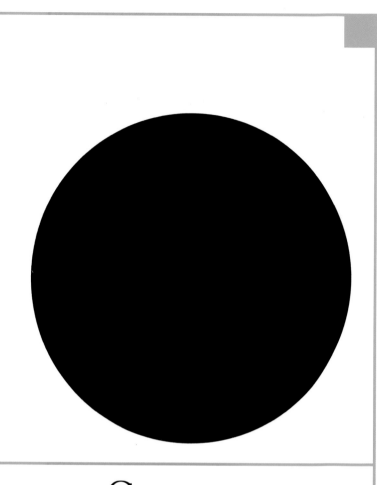

Contents

Note to Parents and Teachers

What's the Time?
is a bright and colorful
early learning book for
you and your child
to share. Packed
with photographs
of everyday activities
and objects, it is an
ideal way to introduce
young children to the
concept of time.

Children first learn about time by relating the hours of a day
to events in their own daily routine. **What's the Time?**
follows a child's typical day, from waking up in the morning
to going to bed at night. Each familiar activity is
related to a time shown on a clock. When you
talk about the pictures together, you can relate
the times shown to your child's own daily experiences.

A special clock with movable hands is included
to encourage children to practice telling time on every
spread. Initially they can simply move the hands to
match the time shown on the pages. As they grow in
confidence, they can try to use the clock to answer
questions about their own lives.

Time to get up

It's seven o'clock in the morning and these children are getting up.

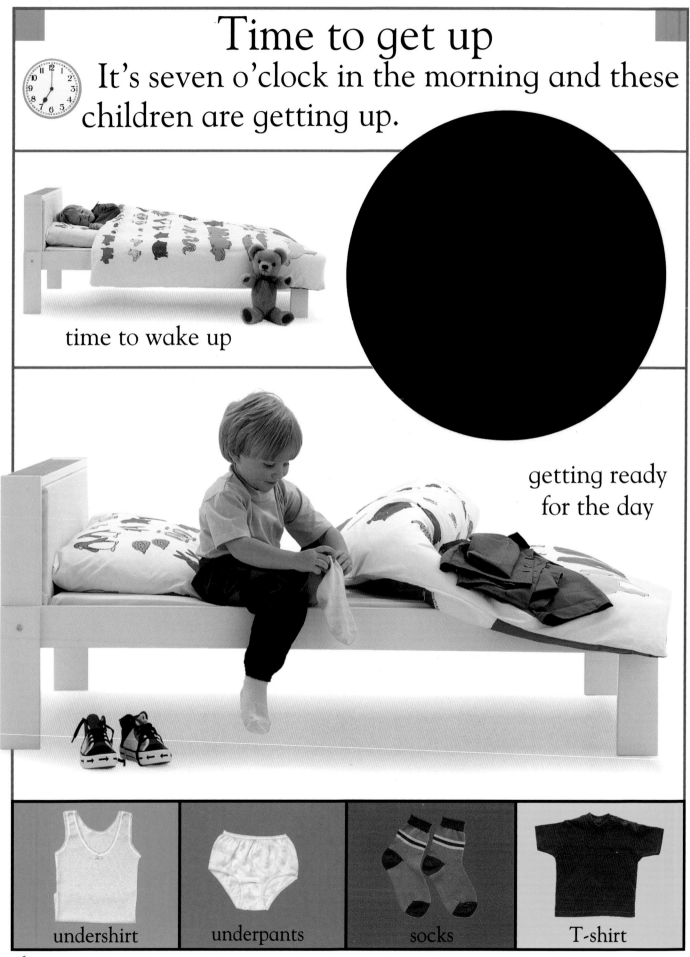

time to wake up

getting ready for the day

undershirt

underpants

socks

T-shirt

brushing teeth

washing

What time do you wake up?

getting dressed

shirt

skirt

pants

shoes

Breakfast time

It's eight o'clock and these children are having their breakfast.

pouring juice

eating breakfast

orange juice

milk

jam

butter

Do you know how
an egg timer works?

What time do you
have your breakfast?

drinking
milk

eating a
banana

feeding the baby

bread

mug

cereal

spoon

9

Playtime

It's nine o'clock and these children are starting to work and play.

drawing

cutting, pasting, and sticking

block

spinning top

crayons

drum

painting

What time do you play?

building
with blocks

reading

| toy airplane | paints and brush | balloon | toy train |

Lunchtime

Twelve o'clock is midday. It is lunchtime for these children.

washing hands

helping make sandwiches

cheese

sandwiches

soup

yogurt

spoon

setting the table

eating lunch

What time do you have your lunch?

sharing a picnic

pizza

cookies

banana

tomato

13

Time to go out

It's two o'clock in the afternoon and these children are going out.

taking the puppy for a walk

playing in the leaves

coat

boots

gloves

scarf

collecting
the groceries

What time do you
go grocery shopping?

paying
at the
checkout

helping unpack

canned tomatoes

apples

peaches

onions

15

Dinnertime

It's six o'clock. Dinnertime! After dinner, these children play.

making a salad

eating dinner

drinking juice

potato and salad

fruit salad

broccoli

corn on the cob

After dinner

What time do you finish your dinner?

playing the violin

petting the puppy

playing a board game

talking to Teddy

television

jigsaw puzzle

marbles

book

17

Bath time

It's seven o'clock in the evening and time for a bath.

brushing hair

washing in the bathtub

hairbrush

comb

sponge

soap

What time do you
take a bath?

drying off
with a
towel

brushing
teeth

getting undressed

shampoo

towel

toothbrush

toothpaste

Bedtime

It's eight o'clock and these children are getting ready for bed.

reading a bedtime story

pajamas

nightshirt

slippers

bathrobe

drying off with a towel

What time do you take a bath?

brushing teeth

getting undressed

shampoo

towel

toothbrush

toothpaste

19

Bedtime

It's eight o'clock and these children are getting ready for bed.

reading a bedtime story

pajamas

nightshirt

slippers

bathrobe

Can you move the hands of the clock to show what time you wake up?

saying goodnight to Teddy

What time do you go to bed?

fast asleep

| mobile | blanket | pillow | teddy bear |